PEOPLE AT
THE CENTER OF

THE INDUSTRIAL REVOLUTION

By SARA WOOTEN

BLACKBIRCH™
PRESS

THOMSON
*
GALE

San Diego • Detroit • New York • San Francisco • Cleveland
New Haven, Conn. • Waterville, Maine • London • Munich

THOMSON

✳ ™

GALE

LIBRARY OF CONGRESS CATALOGING-IN-PUBLICATION DATA

Wooten, Sara McIntosh.
 The industrial revolution / by Sara Wooten.
  p. cm. — (People at the center of:)
 Summary: Profiles three men who were at the center of the industrial revolution— railroad pioneer George Stephenson, textiles industrialist Samuel Slater, and labor leader Samuel Gompers.
 Includes bibliographical references and index.
 ISBN 1-56711-766-X (hardback : alk. paper)
 1. Industrialization—Great Britain—Juvenile literature. 2. Industrialization—United States—Juvenile literature. [1. Industrial revolution. 2. Stephenson, George, 1781-1848. 3. Slater, Samuel, 1768-1835. 4. Gompers, Samuel, 1850-1924.] I. Title. II. Series.

 HD2329.W66 2004
 330.941'07'0922—dc21   2003010092

Printed in United States
10 9 8 7 6 5 4 3 2 1

Contents

PEOPLE AT THE CENTER OF

THE INDUSTRIAL REVOLUTION

On the eve of the Industrial Revolution, life in late-eighteenth-century Great Britain was quite different than it is today. Most people lived in rural areas, where they ate what they farmed and made by hand most of what they needed in daily life. No factories existed to make products. For its economy to develop, Great Britain (soon to unite with Ireland to become the United Kingdom) needed a way to produce goods faster and cheaper, and machines provided the solution.

The textile (cloth) industry was the first to use machinery. Until the mid-1700s, cloth making had hardly changed since the Middle Ages. The spinning wheel operated by one person created one thread at a time, and cloth was handwoven on looms. That practice changed in 1769 when a machine called a water frame was invented that could spin many threads at once. Shortly afterward, in 1785, the power loom automated the process of weaving cloth. Mass production of cloth that could be sold at lower prices resulted, and Great Britain quickly dominated the world's textile industry.

At about the same time, steam power was harnessed to run machines. Before steam, water powered machines, but water was an unpredictable source of energy. Rivers could freeze in winter and dry up in summer, and often it was hard to find running water where work was needed.

The first steam engines pumped seepage water from coal and iron mines so they could be worked. More efficient and versatile steam engines were developed, and by 1775, steam ran machines in textile factories as well as mines. Other industries, such as wool processing and flour milling, quickly followed. With steam engines, goods

Before the invention of the water frame in 1769, cloth was made one thread at a time using a spinning wheel and a loom, just as it had been since the Middle Ages.

were produced faster and could be sold at lower prices, which created increased demand. Great Britain's economy began to explode.

Until 1790, Great Britain was the only country with factories. British manufacturers guarded their factory plans closely, and hoped to maintain their competitive edge in worldwide trade. Nevertheless, in 1789 factory plans came into the United States. One year later, America's first textile factory was in operation, with many others soon to follow.

Meanwhile, innovations in the transportation industry provided faster, more reliable product shipments, and both raw materials and finished products reached their destinations with increased speed and predictability. In 1807, the first commercially successful steamboat made its way up the Hudson River in New York. In 1825, the first steam-powered railway system began operation in Great Britain; a second followed in 1831 in the United States. With more efficient product shipment, industries grew, and the Industrial Revolution gained strength.

The Industrial Revolution began in the late eighteenth century, when the invention of the power loom made mass production of cloth possible in factories such as the one pictured.

The steam locomotive (above) transported factory products to their destinations more quickly and reliably than ever before. The telephone (right) improved communication and the invention of the lightbulb (far right) spurred the growth of the power industry.

Railroads created a need for steel. Superior to iron and wood in strength and durability, steel could be used to make rails as well as bridges and buildings. An inexpensive process was developed to transform iron into steel in 1855, and the steel industry emerged in the United States. The Industrial Revolution expanded further with the first oil well, drilled in 1859. Oil was used to make kerosene for lamps, an improvement over candles and expensive whale oil. Because it was less expensive to produce and transport, oil replaced coal as the basic industrial fuel.

The achievements of American inventors improved communication and created major new industries. With the telegraph in 1837, and the telephone in 1876, messages were communicated instantly. For industry, that meant immediate orders and price quotes, which expanded business and commerce further.

Other inventions also spurred industrial growth. Rubber became a viable product in 1839, and was soon used throughout industry for everything from machinery seals

to conveyor belts and tires. The power industry was born with the invention of the incandescent lightbulb in 1879. Over time, electricity replaced steam to run engines, which led to many new industries that provided convenient electrical consumer products, from fans to vacuum cleaners to Christmas lights.

The Industrial Revolution continued to gain strength with the moving assembly line, first implemented in 1913 for automobile production. Copied throughout industry, it increased productivity and made manufactured products more uniform and less expensive. With the Model T, the first mass-produced automobile, cars became affordable for most Americans, which resulted in a vibrant automobile industry.

The moving assembly line enabled Ford workers to make a Model T in just over an hour and a half. This helped make cars affordable and, by 1927, Ford had sold 15 million Model Ts.

The Industrial Revolution caused life to change quickly and dramatically for people in industrialized nations. Many enjoyed more products, steady jobs, and a higher standard of living. Besides factory work, new white-collar jobs emerged for the management of businesses and employees. and a growing middle class resulted.

Nevertheless, the Industrial Revolution trapped others in poverty and desperation as they moved to cities to take factory jobs. Between 1870 and 1916, almost one-fourth of the American population moved into cities. Immigrants also flocked to the United States with the promise of employment. Cities were not equipped to handle the rapid growth, and drastic housing shortages resulted. Many factory workers were forced to live in dirty, crowded, noisy city tenement housing. Air and water pollution also increased as human and industrial waste went untreated. City air and water smelled foul, garbage littered the streets, and diseases ran unchecked.

Industrial workers were also often bound to dull and dangerous jobs for low wages and long hours. Child labor was another problem, with approximately 2 million children under the age of sixteen employed in industrial jobs by 1900. Children as young as five years old were injured and sometimes killed in industrial accidents. Children might work up to fourteen hours a day, six days a week, around dangerous machinery.

The Industrial Revolution introduced new problems to American society, including a workforce of more than 2 million children (opposite) who toiled in dangerous working conditions. Severe housing shortages in the cities forced many workers to live in rundown tenements (above).

To address these issues, workers formed labor unions to demand higher pay and better working conditions from their employers. Unions also pressured the government to regulate working conditions. To win their battles, unions sometimes decided to strike, and workers refused to return to their jobs until their issues were addressed. Companies responded by hiring strikebreakers to fill jobs during strikes, and violent conflicts often ensued.

By the late 1800s, the United States was the world's industrial leader. For good and ill, the Industrial Revolution changed how and where people lived, worked, communicated, and traveled. Nonindustrialized countries were also affected as increased trade moved the world toward a global economy. With unprecedented innovation, invention, and productivity, the Industrial Revolution changed the world forever.

The youngest of thirteen children, Richard Arkwright was born in 1732 in Preston, England. As an adult he became a barber and wig maker. After several years, however, wigs went out of fashion, and Arkwright needed another means of employment.

In his travels around England to buy hair for wigs, Arkwright met people in the spinning and weaving industries. He learned that demand for cotton fabric was high but the process to make it was slow. Cotton thread was spun by hand, one strand at a time. A spinning machine was needed that could produce multiple cotton threads at once. With technical assistance from a clock maker, Arkwright invented a spinning machine that was easy to operate and produced 128 threads simultaneously. Because the device was powered by water, he called his invention a water frame, which was patented in 1769.

The water frame used rollers that revolved at different speeds to stretch cotton fibers and twist them into yarn. Although Arkwright was not the first to use rollers in a spinning machine, his design improved the process and created stronger, more uniform yarn. In 1771, Arkwright built a spinning factory and hired workers to operate its water frames. Over time, he created an entire industrial village for his workers, complete with cottages, a chapel, and a hotel.

Arkwright's factory was the first facility in which a large group of people worked in a central location on fixed schedules to do specific tasks. The factory operated twenty-three hours a day, and cotton thread became the first product to be mass-produced. Arkwright went on to establish additional mills in northern England and Scotland over the next twenty years. With plentiful cotton yarn, cloth was made faster and the price of English fabric dropped. Soon England was the world's leader in textile production.

With his water frame and factories, Arkwright was responsible for Great Britain's world domination of the textile industry and the economic growth that resulted. Over time, his factory system was copied throughout industry. Arkwright's efforts and innovation brought him wealth and fame. In 1786 he was knighted by King George III. He died in 1792.

Richard Arkwright (opposite) revolutionized the textile industry when he invented the water frame. Arkwright established huge textile mills throughout England, which made that country the world leader in textile production.

JAMES WATT

DESIGNED AND BUILT AN IMPROVED STEAM ENGINE

James Watt was born in 1736 in Scotland, the son of a carpenter. He excelled at mathematics as a child. As an adult, he made scientific instruments for use in fields such as medicine, surveying, and astronomy.

In his work, Watt also became expert at machine repair, and was hired to fix a steam-driven Newcomen pump in 1763. At that time, Newcomens were used widely throughout Great Britain to pump water from coal mines. While he worked to fix the pump, Watt realized how inefficiently the machine operated. It required huge

amounts of coal burned as fuel to heat water that created the steam to run the pump. In addition, most of the steam was wasted while the pump operated. Watt designed and built a new steam engine that pumped faster and used one-fourth the coal needed by the Newcomen. His engine was patented in 1769, which gave him sole rights to profit from his invention for several years.

In widespread use by 1780, Watt's steam engine is considered by many to mark the start of the Industrial Revolution. He went on to build more versatile and powerful versions that could be used to operate machines in industries

James Watt (opposite) designed a steam engine (above) that worked more quickly and used one-fourth the coal needed by its precursor, the Newcomen pump.

other than coal mining. Steam engines quickly became common in textile factories, with eighty-four cotton mills in Great Britain using Watt engines by 1800. Other industries followed, including iron mining, wool processing, and flour milling. Over time, steam power was used to operate machinery in all industries. The use of steam made Great Britain the world's leading industrial power until the late 1800s, when the United States took the lead.

James Watt retired a wealthy and respected man. The standard unit of power, the watt, was named in his honor. He died in 1819.

George Stephenson was born in 1781 and grew up in the coal mining villages of northern England. His father was a mining fireman, who tended the fire that kept steam-driven pumps in operation so the mines stayed dry. George was fascinated with the mine's pumps as a child, and made clay models of them.

Stephenson's interest in pumps continued into adulthood. When a mine pump broke and was disassembled for repair, he studied its parts and made a model to learn how it operated. With this knowledge, Stephenson was hired as an engine man, responsible for the operation and repair of the mine's steam pumps.

Fascinated with steam pumps since childhood, George Stephenson (opposite) designed a steam-powered engine for locomotives (above). Stephenson later helped develop the railway system that linked cities throughout Great Britain.

In Stephenson's day, coal was taken from mines in horse-drawn wagons that ran on iron tracks to docks for shipment to buyers. Stephenson believed steam could be harnessed to run an engine that could transport the coal faster than horses could pull it. He developed a locomotive, or moving steam engine, to test his theory.

First tried in 1814 in Killingworth, England, Stephenson's steam locomotive was noisy and awkward, with a huge boiler and towering funnel to release the steam. Many thought it might blow up. Nevertheless, the machine worked and pulled eight heavy wagons up a slight incline at four miles per hour.

Businessmen began to hire Stephenson to build locomotives and railway systems to link cities throughout Great Britain. The first, completed in 1825, connected Stockton to Darlington. As part of his systems, Stephenson designed the rail beds his locomotives would run on. Achieving highest speed meant keeping the tracks as level as possible. Often that required building bridges over rivers and passes through mountains along the route.

Railways quickly became vital to the thriving British economy. By 1851 more than six thousand miles of railway track connected British cities. Stephenson died in 1848, wealthy and well respected for his contributions to transportation and industry in Great Britain.

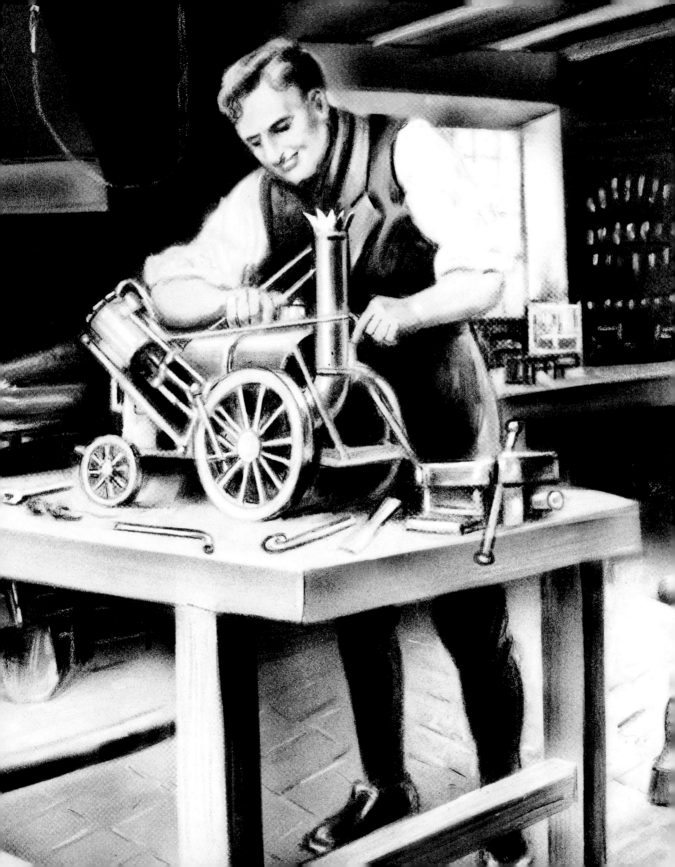

SAMUEL SLATER

BROUGHT COTTON-SPINNING TECHNOLOGY TO AMERICA

Samuel Slater was born in 1768 in Derbyshire, England. By the time he was fifteen years old, Derbyshire had a new cotton factory within walking distance of Samuel's home. For the next six years he worked as an apprentice in the mill, where he learned everything he could about making cotton yarn.

At that time, cotton mills were exclusive to Great Britain and had revolutionized life there. Because factory-made cotton yarn was produced much faster than by hand, the price for cotton cloth dropped dramatically. With high demand worldwide. England dominated the textile industry. Slater realized that cotton mills would be successful in the United States, too, but Great Britain did not want competition from other countries and made it illegal to take factory plans out of the country.

Slater memorized factory plans for the Derbyshire mill, and immigrated to the United States in 1789. There, he teamed with a merchant in Rhode Island who wanted to build a cotton-spinning mill and reproduced the machinery from memory. By December 20, 1790, Slater's mill produced the first factory-made cotton yarn in America, and Slater began to sell yarn to merchants throughout the country.

Samuel Slater (opposite) used his memory of a mill in his hometown of Derbyshire, England, to design America's first cotton-spinning mill (above) in Rhode Island. Slater's introduction of British factory technology jump-started the American textile industry.

At the same time, more cotton mills sprang up in New England. Cotton prices dropped and a new, vital industry was born in the United States. In addition, the factory technology used in the cotton mills was applied to other industries over time.

Samuel Slater's knowledge and ingenuity set the Industrial Revolution in motion in America. He died in 1835, a wealthy and respected man.

Robert Fulton was born in Lancaster County, Pennsylvania, in 1765. He was known as a daydreamer because he could not keep his mind on his schoolwork. Fulton also loved to paint, and became an artist as an adult. Although he was somewhat successful, he could not sell enough paintings to earn a living. Over time he decided inventions would be more profitable.

Designed by Robert Fulton (opposite), the Clermont (above) successfully sailed up the Hudson River from New York City to Albany in 1807. Fulton's creation of the first working steamboat allowed faster transportation of goods.

In Fulton's day, goods were transported over rough, poor roads, or over water in barges or boats. Both ways were slow. Fulton knew that steam-powered boats would make transportation much faster, so at thirty-six he decided to build one. After many sketches, he designed a large boat to hold lots of cargo, with a sleek shape so the boat would move efficiently through water. Inside, a steam engine provided the boat's power.

In 1803, Fulton's first successful steamboat paddled along the Seine River in Paris, France, where Fulton had moved in 1797. Steam poured from its smoke-stack as the boat slowly began to move upstream on its own power, to the amazement of onlookers. At four and a half miles per hour. Fulton's steamboat moved much faster than a barge.

In the United States three years later, Fulton repeated his earlier success with a new steamboat, the *Clermont*. Many doubted the boat would work and called it Fulton's Folly. Others thought it would blow up from the steam's pressure, Yet the *Clermont's* journey was a success. It traveled 150 miles from New York City up the Hudson River to Albany, New York, on August 17, 1807.

The *Clermont's* trip marked a new era in transportation. With steamboats, product shipments were no longer delayed by raging river currents or lack of wind. Steamboats could move upstream almost as fast as downstream. Faster, more depend-able product shipments meant more business for American industries. By the time Fulton died in 1815, the steamboat had become a popular and profitable way to ship goods in the United States.

SAMUEL F.B. MORSE

INVENTED THE TELEGRAPH AND MORSE CODE

Samuel Morse was born in 1791 in Charlestown, Massachusetts. Although he graduated from Yale College, studies did not interest Samuel. He wanted to be a painter, but over time he realized he could not support himself as an artist.

On a transatlantic voyage to the United States after a trip to Europe to study painting, Morse had a chance conversation about electricity with another passenger, who told Morse of the discovery that electricity could travel through wire. That information made Morse begin to think that electricity could be used to transmit sound through wire as well.

Samuel Morse (opposite) invented the telegraph in 1837. Messages written in his code of dots and dashes that represent letters of the alphabet (above) could be sent by wire, opening the world to rapid long-distance communication.

At the time, most communication consisted of hand-delivered written messages. A message could take days or weeks to reach its destination. Morse knew that the development of a faster communication system would bring him financial success and allow him to paint once again.

With technical assistance from friends, in 1837 Morse demonstrated the first successful telegraph, a device that sends messages long distances over wire. He also created a code made up of dots and dashes that represent each letter of the alphabet. To send a message, a telegraph operator used the code to tap each letter of the message on the telegraph. The code was transmitted over wire, received by another telegraph at its destination, and translated back into English.

In 1843, the U.S. Congress authorized funds for the first telegraph system, which was built the next year. It ran from Washington, D.C., to Baltimore, Maryland, with electrical wire strung on poles between the two cities. The project was a success, and the new communication system quickly spread in America. Telegraph messages soon became vital to business communication. For new American industries, the telegraph meant price quotes and product orders could be relayed much faster. Business efficiency increased dramatically, which encouraged continued industrial growth.

For more than forty years Morse's telegraph was the world's foremost method for long-distance communication. His invention brought him fame, wealth, and numerous awards. He died in 1872.

CHARLES GOODYEAR

INVENTED VULCANIZED RUBBER

Charles Goodyear was born in 1800 in New Haven. Connecticut. His father, a miller, made buttons and other household products. Charles joined his father's business, but when it failed, he needed a new livelihood.

Goodyear became an inventor, and in 1832 he turned his attention to rubber, produced from the sap of tropical trees in South America and Asia. Its unusual properties included elasticity and resistance to water. Goodyear saw potential in the product, but there was one problem: temperature. Heat made it sticky and melt, and cold made it harden and crack. Goodyear wanted to make rubber useful, so he began trial-and-error experiments to solve the problem.

Goodyear's experiments became an obsession, and for years he failed. Meanwhile, his family suffered extreme poverty and ridicule. With limited income, Goodyear sold household furnishings and books to fund his experiments. His debts mounted, and he was sent to debtor's prison numerous times.

Finally, in 1839, Goodyear accidentally spilled a mixture of rubber and sulfur on a hot stove. Surprisingly, it did not melt. In fact, the rubber remained strong and flexible, despite exposure to heat or cold. The chemical process he developed to treat crude rubber, called vulcanization, made possible countless uses for the new product.

Rubber was first used to make waterproof shoes, hats, and coats, along with carriage covers and life preservers. Over time, rubber became vital in industry. Rubber seals were critical for industrial machinery because they kept machine parts tightly connected and free from moisture. In addition, factories used rubber conveyor belts for assembly lines. The rise of the automobile industry created still more uses for rubber in belts, tubing, and tires. With Goodyear's discovery, rubber became a core industry in the United States and throughout the world.

Soon after Charles Goodyear (opposite) developed the vulcanization process that makes crude rubber (above) strong and flexible, rubber became a major industry in the United States and the rest of the world.

Charles Goodyear patented his vulcanization process in 1844, which established him as its inventor and gave him sole rights to profit from his invention for several years. Over time, he made a lot of money from his invention, but he used most of it to research new uses for rubber. He died penniless in 1860.

Alexander Graham Bell was born in 1847 in Edinburgh, Scotland. His father and grandfather were well-known speech teachers; his mother was deaf. When he was a young man, Bell settled in Boston, Massachusetts, where he taught deaf students. Over time, he turned his attention to sound research.

By the time he was twenty-nine years old, Bell had worked for two years on one problem: how to send actual human speech through wire from one place to another. Groundwork for the telephone had been laid with the telegraph, invented in 1837. Telegraph messages were converted into code, sent as electrical signals through wire, and translated back into English.

Alexander Graham Bell's telephone (above) quickly became one of history's most important technological advances. Influenced by his deaf mother and speech-teacher father, Bell (opposite) had a lifelong fascination with sound.

Bell's project was more complicated than telegraph code. Sound waves had to be transformed into electrical signals, transmitted, and then changed back into words. Bell experimented and sketched new designs while his assistant, Thomas Watson, built models. With hundreds of notebooks filled with records of failed trials, Bell knew that each failure brought him closer to success.

On March 10, 1876, in Boston, Massachusetts, Bell used his latest telephone model to send a message: "Mr. Watson, come here. I want to see you." Within moments, Watson appeared before Bell and repeated the message. The telephone was born that day, and world communication changed forever.

For the next few years Bell promoted his invention throughout the United States, and the telephone industry emerged. Electrical wire was strung throughout the country, and factories were built to make telephones. Businesses immediately saw the telephone's advantages. Orders for products and raw materials could be placed quickly, without delays imposed by the more cumbersome telegraph. Better communication reinforced the continued expansion of the Industrial Revolution.

By 1917, most of the nation was connected with telephone service and Bell's invention became one of the most important technological advancements of all time. He died in 1922.

THOMAS EDISON

INVENTED THE PHONOGRAPH AND ELECTRIC LIGHTING

As a boy, Thomas Edison was not considered a good student. His mind wandered and he found it difficult to concentrate on his studies. Born in 1847 in Milan, Ohio, Edison was curious and liked to experiment, especially with chemicals.

As an adult, Edison first worked as a telegraph operator. In his spare time he pursued a wide variety of inventions. By 1876, Edison was a full-time inventor, and built a research laboratory in Menlo Park, New Jersey. During his amazing career there he became known as the Wizard of Menlo Park.

Over his lifetime, Edison invented more than one thousand new products. He improved Alexander Graham Bell's telephone and invented the phonograph, which could record sound and play it back again. In 1878, he began to experiment with the electric lightbulb.

Electric lights were available in Edison's time, but they were too bright and hot for indoor use. Instead, people used candles, oil lamps, or gas to light their homes. Edison needed to find a material for the filament, or thin strand inside the bulb, that would glow but not burn up when electricity flowed through it. After thousands of failed trials, in 1879 Edison found that carbonized thread worked. The result was an inexpensive lightbulb with soft, long-lasting light. He then created a workable lighting system with light switches and sockets, along with giant electric generators, or dynamos,

Thomas Edison (opposite) invented more than one thousand products, including the phonograph (above). Edison's invention of the lightbulb created a great demand for electricity and a need for the power industry.

that could deliver huge amounts of electricity over wires to users.

Edison's lighting system spread quickly into homes and businesses. With demand for electricity came the power-generating industry. By 1898, more than three thousand power companies supported users throughout America.

Edison's practical electric lighting system changed industry forever. Candles and expensive kerosene were replaced with electric lights, which were cleaner and safer to use. Edison's work also led to a wide array of electrically powered consumer products such as refrigerators, ovens, and sewing machines. In industry, electricity soon replaced steam as the primary power source for machinery.

Edison became one of the most famous men in the world. Over his lifetime he was granted more patents, or rights as an inventor, by the U.S. Patent Office than any other person. When he died in 1931, Americans turned off their electric lights for one minute in his honor.

Edison, pictured here in his laboratory, achieved success and fame despite the fact that he was considered a poor student in his youth.

ANDREW CARNEGIE

DEVELOPED THE AMERICAN STEEL INDUSTRY

The son of a weaver, Andrew Carnegie was born in Scotland in 1835. His father made linen cloth by hand. By the time Andrew was twelve years old, new steam-powered textile factories had replaced individual workshops in Scotland. Andrew's father needed work, so he brought his family to America, and settled near Pittsburgh, Pennsylvania.

Andrew went to work in a cotton factory, and later as a telegraph messenger boy. Over time, he learned to send messages on the telegraph. At seventeen, he was hired to operate the telegraph office of the Pennsylvania Railroad. He rose to become manager of the railroad's Pittsburgh division.

Carnegie knew that steel would be needed to build railroads and bridges. Steel was made from iron, but the conversion process was very expensive. In 1855, British engineer Henry Bessemer had developed a cheaper process and early steel works were built in England. Carnegie resigned from the railroad in

Andrew Carnegie's development of the steel industry (above) brought the United States to the forefront of steel production worldwide and made Carnegie himself (opposite) one of the richest men in the world.

1865, and eventually decided to enter the steel industry. In 1873, he and several partners built America's first large-scale steel plant, which used Bessemer's process.

Steel was used to make everything from railroad ties, bridges, and steamships to agricultural equipment. Carnegie's development of the steel industry made the United States the world's leading steel producer. With cheap, abundant steel, American industries grew. As businessmen built more factories that produced more goods, the Industrial Revolution surged forward.

By 1901, Andrew Carnegie was one of the wealthiest men in the world. He sold his company to industrialist and banker J.P. Morgan for $400 million and it became the core of the giant U.S. Steel Corporation. Carnegie then gave away much of his fortune, because he believed that wealth should be used to help others. One of his most enduring legacies was a network of more than twenty-eight hundred public libraries throughout the world. Carnegie died in 1919.

JOHN D. ROCKEFELLER

DEVELOPED AND STANDARDIZED THE U.S. OIL INDUSTRY

John Davison Rockefeller was born in 1839 near Ithaca, New York. With an early interest in business, he sold candy for profit to his brothers and sisters. As a teenager he took bookkeeping classes, and began work as an accountant in Cleveland, Ohio.

In 1859, the world's first oil well was drilled in Titusville, Pennsylvania. Crude oil could be refined into kerosene to light lamps. Rockefeller invested money in an oil refinery, and gradually became involved in its management. Under his direction, the company acquired control of every aspect of the refinery business: drilling, refining, selling, and shipping. That way, all profits stayed in the company. In 1870, Rockefeller's company became the Standard Oil Company of Ohio, the largest refinery in Cleveland.

John D. Rockefeller (opposite) became America's first billionaire after he created a monopoly in the oil industry (above) that undercut his competitors' prices and forced them out of business.

Rockefeller then proceeded to eliminate his competition. He commonly undercut his competitors' prices, and forced them out of business. He also attacked companies that did business with his competitors. When necessary, Rockefeller resorted to more cutthroat tactics, such as bribery, physical threats, and sabotage. One by one, other oil companies either joined Standard Oil or went bankrupt. By 1880, Rockefeller controlled 95 percent of America's oil business. Standard Oil became one of the first U.S. monopolies, or companies with almost no competition.

Rockefeller thought industry consolidation provided standardization and stability to a new and unstable industry. The public, however, was outraged by Rockefeller's brutal business tactics, and he became known as the most hated man in America. Regardless, Rockefeller's development and standardization of the oil industry made one of the largest and most important industries in the United States.

Rockefeller retired in 1897, America's first billionaire. He then turned his attention to the Rockefeller Foundation, which gave away hundreds of millions of dollars for education, medical research, and the arts. By the time Rockefeller died in 1937, laws had eliminated monopolies in the United States, and Standard Oil no longer controlled the oil industry in America.

Henry Ford, born in 1863, grew up on a farm near Dearborn, Michigan. With a strong interest in machinery, he left home at seventeen for Detroit. There he worked in a series of industrial jobs as a mechanic and engineer.

Fascinated with engines, Ford wanted to develop a gasoline-powered model light enough to run on wheels. After five years of effort, he produced his first gasoline-powered automobile in 1896. Soon afterward, he began to make cars full-time.

In 1903, Ford bought a small manufacturing plant in Detroit and opened the Ford Motor Company. His first product was the Model A, a vehicle that could operate at thirty miles per hour. Ford's Model T was unveiled in 1908. Ford standardized the Model T so it could be produced faster and sold at a lower price than the Model A.

Ford's cars were well received by the public, but they were still too expensive for many people. To produce them more cheaply, he created a moving assembly line in 1913. At that time, assembly lines were in limited use, but Ford's moving assembly line made the process more efficient. Instead of building a car in one spot as workers added parts to it, Ford's process kept workers stationary while the car moved. Each worker performed a few simple tasks as each car passed by. With the moving assembly line, production time for the Model T dropped from 12.5 hours to 2.5 hours. By 1914, a Model T was made in just over 1.5 hours.

With efficient production, Ford reduced the price of his cars. He also established a credit system to purchase them. With more affordable prices and small monthly payments, the Model T became the most popular car in the world, with 15 million sold by 1927.

Transportation changed forever with Ford's automobiles. To meet the public's demand for cars, a new automobile industry emerged in the United States. In addition, Ford's innovative production methods influenced leaders in other industries and many copied his moving assembly line. As a result the number of American-made products increased

In failing health, Ford put his grandson in charge of the Ford Motor Company in 1945. Ford then turned his attention to the development of the Ford Foundation, which became one of the largest charitable foundations in the United States. The foundation supported schools, museums, and hospitals. Henry Ford died in 1947.

Henry Ford revolutionized the automobile industry by making cars affordable. With decreased prices and a credit payment system, his Model T became the most popular car in the world.

SAMUEL GOMPERS

FOUNDED THE AMERICAN FEDERATION OF LABOR

Samuel Gompers was born in England in 1850, the eldest son of a cigar maker. Samuel began to learn the highly skilled craft of cigar making when he was ten. In 1863, the Gompers family moved to America and settled in New York City.

As a cigar maker, Gompers joined the local cigar-makers union. He became known for his cigar-making skill, along with his leadership qualities and ability to give effective speeches. By 1875, he had become president of his local union. In 1881, Gompers and other union members formed a national union called the Federation of Organized Trades and Labor Unions of the United States and Canada. Its purpose was to educate and influence the public on workers' issues, and encourage Congress to pass laws that would improve working conditions. In 1886, the organization was renamed the American Federation of Labor (AFL).

The AFL comprised mainly skilled workers, in contrast with another national union, the Knights of Labor, established in 1869, that admitted both skilled and unskilled laborers. Gompers believed the AFL would have increased power because skilled workers would be more difficult to replace in a strike. Under Gompers's leadership, the AFL favored collective bargaining between employers and workers, rather than strikes. With collective bargaining, representatives from each side discussed their needs to try to reach a peaceful agreement.

By the late 1800s, factory workers (above) began to form labor unions to demand better wages and working conditions. As head of the American Federation of Labor, Samuel Gompers (opposite) helped win significant rights for workers and worked to regulate child labor.

By 1904, the AFL was the strongest labor organization in the United States, with more than 1.5 million members. The organization won significant rights for workers and successfully supported laws that shortened work hours, regulated child labor, and required employers to pay workers for job-related accidents. Except for one year, Gompers led the AFL from 1881 until his death in 1924.

MARY HARRIS JONES

LABOR MOVEMENT LEADER

Mary Harris was born in 1830 in Ireland. When she was seven, her family moved to Canada, where her father worked for the railroad. Harris grew up to teach school and marry George E. Jones, an ironworker. As an active union member, he joined with other ironworkers to get better pay and working conditions.

When Jones was thirty-one, her husband and four children died suddenly of yellow fever. She moved to Chicago and was struck by disaster again when she lost everything in the Great Chicago Fire of 1871. She turned to the Knights of Labor, America's largest labor union at the time, for shelter and assistance.

Grateful for their help and sympathetic toward their goals, Jones joined the Knights of Labor in their fight for workers' rights. She traveled to coal mines, railroads, factories, and mills from Pennsylvania to Alabama to encourage union membership and give speeches for better working conditions. Just five feet tall, she typically wore a black dress with a lace collar, and became a familiar sight at labor gatherings and demonstrations. Jones, or Mother Jones as she came to be called, repeatedly put herself in danger as she led workers in strikes against their employers. She persevered against threats, insults, and injury, and was even jailed several times because she led strikes.

Mary Harris Jones (opposite), who became known as Mother Jones, campaigned tirelessly for workers' rights. Jones also brought public attention to the plight of working children (above), who often toiled in dangerous places like mines and factories.

Jones also recognized the power of publicity to educate people about dangerous working conditions and the effects of child labor. She used speeches, rallies, and demonstrations to attract the press so her message was heard. In 1903, she led a 125-mile march of two hundred child workers from Philadelphia, Pennsylvania, to President Theodore Roosevelt's summer home in Oyster Bay, New York, to publicize their cause.

The impact of Mother Jones on the labor movement was immense. She helped recruit new union members, and with her assistance, the Knights of Labor reached its peak membership of seven hundred thousand in 1886. By the time Jones died in 1930, child labor laws had been passed in a number of states, due in large part to her efforts.

JANE ADDAMS

Born into a wealthy Quaker family in 1860, Jane Addams grew up in Cedarville, Illinois. Her father was much respected in Cedarville, and served as a state senator. Well educated, Addams chose not to marry but to dedicate herself to public service.

Addams decided to start a home in Chicago to address the needs of poor factory workers. In 1889 she acquired a shabby mansion called Hull House in one of Chicago's most dilapidated residential neighborhoods. From there, she established programs to assist and benefit the neighborhood residents.

Jane Addams (opposite) founded Hull House (above), a center for programs to help the poor, in a rundown neighborhood of Chicago. Addams's advocacy of child labor laws led to the Illinois Factory Act, which limited the number of hours children could work.

Once a wealthy area of Chicago, the Hull House neighborhood had declined. It was rundown, filthy, and overcrowded. Low rents there attracted many immigrants, many of whom could not speak English. Most worked in low-paying factory jobs. Addams was determined to make a difference in their lives.

Over the next forty-six years, Addams used Hull House as her base to put her belief in social reform in practice. She established a kindergarten for the neighborhood youngsters, a child care center, and clubs for the area youth. English and literacy classes were held for adults, along with vocational and craft training. She provided food for those in need and medical care for the sick. She also found jobs and homes for many desperate people, and even became a garbage inspector to ensure regular trash removal in the neighborhood. At the same time, Addams promoted the programs at Hull House to raise funds for operating expenses.

Through her work, Addams realized the disadvantages and dangers of child labor. She vigorously promoted child labor legislation in Illinois, and in 1893, her efforts resulted in the Illinois Factory Act, one of America's first child labor laws to limit the number of hours children could work. In 1931, Addams was awarded the Nobel Peace Prize. By the time she died in 1935, Jane Addams was one of the world's best-known, most admired women.

1769	Richard Arkwright patents the water frame, an improvement on the cotton–machine. James Watt patents an efficient, reliable steam engine.
1771	Richard Arkwright establishes the first cotton–spinning factory in Cromford, England.
1785	The power loom is invented, which mechanizes cloth weaving.
1790	The first textile factory is established in the United States.
1807	Robert Fulton's steamboat, the *Clermont,* becomes the first commercially successful steamboat.
1814	George Stephenson introduces the first reliable steam locomotive.
1825	George Stephenson opens the first regular rail service between Stockton and Darlington, England.
1837	Samuel F.B. Morse invents the telegraph.
1839	Charles Goodyear vulcanizes rubber.
1844	The first telegraph system is built, which links Washington, D.C., and Baltimore, Maryland.
1855	Henry Bessemer develops an affordable process to convert iron to steel.
1859	The first oil well is drilled in Titusville, Pennsylvania.
1869	The Noble and Holy Order of the Knights of Labor is founded.
1873	The first large-scale steel mill is established in the United States.
1876	Alexander Graham Bell invents the telephone.
1879	Thomas Edison invents the first practical incandescent lightbulb.
1881	The Federation of Organized Trades and Labor Unions of the United States and Canada is formed.
1889	Hull House is established in Chicago, Illinois, to address social needs.
1903	Mary Harris Jones leads two hundred children in a march to publicize the hazards of child labor.
1908	Henry Ford introduces the Model T automobile.
1913	Henry Ford introduces the moving assembly line to produce automobiles.

The world's first oil well (pictured), drilled in 1859, was in Titusville, Pennsylvania. The modern petroleum industry was just one of many launched during the Industrial Revolution.

FOR FURTHER INFORMATION

BOOKS

Michael Burgan, *Henry Ford*. Milwaukee, WI: World Almanac Library, 2002.

Christopher Collier and James Lincoln Collier, *The Rise of Industry, 1860–1900*. New York: Benchmark, 2000.

Jodine Mayberry, *Business Leaders Who Built Financial Empires*. Austin, TX: Raintree Steck-Vaughn, 1994.

Anita Louise McCormick, *The Industrial Revolution in American History*. Springfield, NJ: Enslow, 1998.

Christopher Simonds, *Samuel Slater's Mill and the Industrial Revolution*. Englewood Cliffs, NJ: Silver Burdett, 1990.

Anna Sproule, *James Watt, Master of the Steam Engine*. Woodbridge, CT: Blackbirch, 2001.

Thomas Streissguth, *Legendary Labor Leaders*. Minneapolis. MN: Oliver, 1998.

WEBSITES

The Industrial Revolution
www.fordham.edu
This site contains resources from the Internet Modern History Sourcebook.

Kidinfo
www.kidinfo.com
This site provides links to essays, articles, time lines, and biographies related to the Industrial Revolution.

Steam Engine Library
www.history.rochester.edu
This site is a collection of resources about the steam engine and the Industrial Revolution.

ABOUT THE AUTHOR

Sara Wooten has worked as a teacher and a technical writer. She lives in the Midwest with her husband and a variety of pets. She has also written *Martha Stewart, America's Lifestyle Expert* for Blackbirch Press.